Postcards from Soweto

Mokone Molete

JACANA

The author would like to express profound gratitude for the faith – in the project and the author – shown by Ipuseng Kotsokoane, who ensured that this book sees the light of day. The painstaking efforts in getting the book to the bookstores is well appreciated. I would also like to thank Mongadi Matata for his comments. They were noted, fiercely debated, and appreciated.

First published by Jacana Media (Pty) Ltd in 2007

10 Orange Street
Sunnyside
Auckland Park 2092
South Africa
+2711 628 3200
www.jacana.co.za

© Mokone Molete, 2007

ISBN 978-1-77009-369-0

Cover design by miss sweden
Set in Sabon 12/15pt
Printed by CTP Book Printers, Cape
Job No. 000483

See a complete list of Jacana titles at www.jacana.co.za

Prologue

Sixty per cent of the events that follow are true. The remaining forty per cent are poetic licence. Certain names have been changed to protect the innocent – namely, myself. These missives are the postcards I should have written as I grew up in Diepkloof, a nondescript township in Soweto. They are pastiches of life as I remember it, lived with my friends, at home and at school. Most of the events in this book took place while I was growing up.

The events related in these postcards are true. They are meant to be enjoyed for what they are: vignettes from the past of a very impressionable young Sowetan. To better appreciate them, a few pointers are necessary. First, let us be clear that this collection is not a socio-historical treatise on the lives of black people in the townships. The (embellished) experiences recorded here may or may not be typical of life as it was in the townships. My contemporaries may well have had different experiences.

Notwithstanding, some occurrences were common experiences in those days. During my formative years, being beaten by parents and teachers was *de rigueur* and I have no views on their 'badness' or otherwise. That is simply how things were, and that is how we accepted them. Period. Homosexuals were at best derided as social deviants and at worst 'sickos' who deserved to be ostracised. This will help you understand Mzi's reaction to Cousy in 'Cousy'.

Lastly, *Postcards from Soweto* needs to be enjoyed for what it is: recollections of a middle-aged hack reminiscing rather romantically about days gone by. As I have mentioned, some of the events are true, especially those that relate to my family. Some of my friends may see bits and pieces of themselves in these pages. Fellows, don't you think this calls for another helluva *phuza* drinking session?

Contents

Home

Thola, I am talking to you

When I was young, getting your backside whipped was a rite of passage that we accepted, like the rain and the sun, as a way of life. I mean, even people who had cool parents, like Ricky, reported getting a whack now and then. Purists will groan at news of this 'abuse'. Ah well, what I can say? As the elders used to tell us: this is for your own good.

'When Sello was sentenced to death for the many crimes he had committed, including murder, he told the court he wanted to whisper something to his mother,' Mama would tell us. Sello's mother was brought closer to him in the witness box. And right there, in front of everyone, Mama told the wide-eyed bunch of us, he bit his mother's ear off. 'That is for not chiding me when I got myself into mischief,' Sello said to his mother. 'So there is a lesson for you. When I punish you, it means I love you,' Mama concluded. And what love it was. We swapped notes about this kind of love.

Oscar said his mother was a thrower. '*Ma-auti* [gents], I make sure that when I am in trouble

1

there is a long, long distance between me and my ma. She *goois* [throws] everything, *ek sê*. Pots, brooms, kettles – whatever is at hand. Last week she dispatched a whole glass of Coca-Cola on my shirt. *Jislaaik*, and I had just ironed that shirt, *and* I was thirsty,' he added, incredulity painted all over his face. His crime? 'I had told Ma that I would wash the dishes after I came back from Zone 5' (where we knew his Lindi lived). *"Ha o ntlhomphe. Ke re o sebetse ene o re nywe-nywe.* [You are disrespectful. I ask you to do some work and you give me lip.] *Sies."* And whoosh! Who would have thought she would waste a cold glass of Coca-Cola like that?' So that's how Oscar went to see Lindi wearing Billy's shirt. When he returned, his father finished what his mother had started.

Billy's defence was also distance, and his mother's long talons were her weapons of destruction. He bore the evidence all over his body – bar his face. He was pockmarked with scars where his mother had let rip with her fingernails each time he committed some infraction. We resorted to calling him Billy 2, because he wore double shirts, double trousers and double everything else, so that in times of trouble, he would be well protected. Fortunately for Billy 2, he grew into a bulky fellow, encouraged by the many clothes he wore, we believed. This forced his mother to resort to screaming and shouting, which had none of the desired effect of changing his behaviour. Billy 2 said his mother eventually believed that he was deaf.

My Mama was an all-rounder: she *moered* [beat up] him, she threw things, she cajoled and she lectured him. She never swore, though. 'Why... (*wham!*) did you go... (*wham!*) playing at the mine dumps (*wham!*)?'

As each part of the question was punctuated by a slap, I tried to answer: 'Ma, it was...'

And then, *wham!* 'Thola, shaddup! Don't you answer back when I am talking to you!' *Wham!* 'Go and clean the *stoep*.' *Wham!*

To this very day, Mama denies right in front of my children that she ever beat us.

So you are a man

It must be the testosterone. A man – to be truthful, a boy – reaches a point in his life when he thinks he is *da man* and very invincible. The problem, though, is that we test this belief against the worst of opponents: someone much bigger or much older.

In truth, the consolation is that it has happened to all of us, and seemingly more or less around the same age.

That is, around the time when the voice has just about cracked, and pubic hair is making its first appearance. And were it not for Pitso, we wouldn't have known that we shared this generational affliction.

'Jeez!' we chorused as he joined us for a pre-class game of soccer in the school grounds.

'What happened?' we enquired, referring to the shiner that normally would have been displayed with pride. You know, the one that says to your friends: you think I have had it bad, you should

4

see what the other guy looks like. Unfortunately, as it turned out, the other guy in Pitso's encounter was unmarked.

'It was my old man, gents,' he began. 'Last night, he started his nonsense again. Around eight o'clock he wanted me to go and buy him cigarettes. I decided to hell with this; I am grown up now and no one is going to boss me around, especially when I was listening to a story on the radio' (these were pre-TV days).

We edged closer. 'And then?'

'He asked me if I was refusing to be sent to the shops. "*Ka bohla,*" I mumbled in protest. He then left me alone and I thought, Ja, now he knows I am a man and he won't mess with me anymore. It was now the turn of the others in the house to be bossed around.'

'And then?'

'*Ag*, after listening to the story I went outside to the toilet. *Ei*, sonny. I was feeling so good to finally have sorted out my old man. I was even whistling.'

Pitso proffered a smile through his pain.

'When I stepped back into the house, the old bugger was hiding behind the door and he grabbed me by the neck and – *doof!* – a straight right, directly at my face.'

'Yooo!' we yelled out in sympathy.

'I was ding-dong,' Pitso remarked.

'He said, "So you are a man, let's fight." Another right. *Doof!* (We all winced.) "This rubbish of

yours thinks he is a man and yet he can't fight."
He then turned me around, kicked my backside
and told me to go and get his cigarettes.'

'*Ei*, you are lucky,' Sy-Sy said as he took his
shirt off, displaying a spectacular map of scars.

'Look at me. Same thing. But you know what
my father did? He waited until I went to sleep.
2am, I feel the blankets being ripped off my bed.
En ek is kaalgat [and I was naked]. The door
closed and my dad started raining his belt all over
me. "*Kom*," he said, "*jy is mos 'n man.*" [Come,
you are a man, aren't you?] *Wha! Wha! Wha!* He
kept going. "*Kom*," he says, "*jy is mos 'n man.*"
Ei monna [Hey guys], I couldn't do anything. I
just had to cover my parcels [private parts]. I was
screaming "Sorry!" and my mother was pounding
at the door, which was locked.'

'*Tjotjo*,' we offered our sympathies, having
forgotten about Pitso's fresh wounds.

'*Wha! Wha! Wha!* And only when he was
satisfied, did my father unlock the door, and say
to me, "*Jou moer* [You arse]."

Then he left the room. I can still hear my mother
screaming at him, saying he was a beast. For once
I was not interested in their argument. My body
was sore all over,' a morose Sy-Sy concluded.

And then everyone had a tale to tell. Gordon
was choked by his old man. Jeff's father was
an ex-boxer and said they should shape up; Jeff
came off second best in a contest where there
was only one outcome. Pele said his old man had
dunked his head in a bath full of water. Only Jakie

had nothing to declare – he lived alone with his
grandmother.

Abuti Beef

Very few characters are so nonchalant about life as Abuti Beef, and yet so lovable. I did not know him well, but one of the things I do remember was that the day my mother received news of his departure from this earth, she wailed. I had never, up to that point, seen my mother cry. As with many mortals, upon his demise stories of his rather gung-ho life started surfacing – all true. His name, for one. Whenever there was a traditional feast, you could rely on Abuti Beef to offer his services – freely and reliably. He mastered the art of slaughtering the beasts that would be prepared on these special occasions. If it were a cow to go into the big three-legged pots (*drie-voet* pots we used to call them), Abuti Beef would smack his lips in anticipation. 'Ah, beef this time,' he would declare. Hence the nickname.

Abuti Beef was tall, a gangly six foot-something. He had broad shoulders, a flat nose that made him look menacing, and his laughter came in short, loud bursts that were very infectious. He would never win a Mr Looks contest, but folks, his heart made up for it. 'God can't give you everything,' said my mother when it came to describing Abuti Beef.

He was the same height as my old man, who was known as Uncle Wales to my mother, and Bra Wally to his friends. Legend has it my dad was so nicknamed because he was as tall as the Prince of Wales (the man who later abdicated when he wanted to marry Mrs Simpson). The fact that Abuti Beef had the same build as my old man made it unnecessary for him to bring any spare clothes when he came to sleep over at our house. He knew that something – in fact everything – in Uncle Wales's wardrobe fitted him. Similarly, when my dad visited my grandparents in Alexandra Township, where Abuti Beef lived, he would not be left cold or wet should the weather change and he needed a change of clothing.

As it happened, when Abuti Beef left for the Pearly Gates there was confusion as to which were his clothes and which were my dad's. Tradition demands that after a certain time has passed, the clothes of a dead person are divided up between his or her surviving relatives. The problem was solved, I seem to remember, by my dad getting the biggest heap of Abuti Beef's clothes!

Abuti Beef's visits to our house were also memorable for other reasons. I very rarely remember him visiting during the day. He always came at night. And more often than not he was with Abuti Godfrey, a cousin on my mother's side. Abuti Godfrey was half Abuti Beef's height, and his shortness was exaggerated by the fact that he was hunch-backed. What a sight this pair made. Loud, always cheerful, these two were always welcome at any time of day or night.

Abuti Beef was no Einstein, his talents lying in his being handy. As such, he was the trusted fixer-upper in the family. Ramogolo Mampane, an uncle, gave Abuti Beef the use of his motorbike to travel between Alexandra Township and Diepkloof, where he went to high school. Many a time, we were told, Abuti Beef forgot the motorbike at the local bar where he often went after classes. And back in those halcyon days no one bothered to nick his transport.

His mother, Rakgadi Mamiki, had a car, and Abuti Beef played chauffeur, as she didn't have a driver's licence. One Sunday, Abuti Beef, not normally known for his sartorial elegance, dressed up and preened himself after giving the car a great valet service. Just then, his mother asked to be taken to Tladi, to visit Ramogolo Mampane, his uncle – her mother's brother. Uncharacteristically, Abuti Beef nixed his mother's request. My granddad was summoned to sort the situation out and he, not known for taking nonsense from anyone, made it clear to Abuti Beef that refusing to take his mother was as good as signing his death warrant. Soon afterwards a happy party of Rakgadi, cousins Ausi Nono and Ausi Manki, and a very grumpy Abuti Beef set off for Soweto – normally a trip that he would look forward to, seeing that Ramogolo Mampane had a shop and a generous heart. But Abuti Beef was in no mood for socialising with his relatives. In fact he spent most of the visit in Tladi buffing and rebuffing the car. The visit over, Rakgadi asked to take the wheel as she was practising for her driver's licence. Abuti Beef declined her request until she reminded him that his grandfather was still alive. Abuti Beef reluctantly handed over the keys.

'Turn left,' he told Rakgadi as they left Ramogolo's house at the back of the shop.

'Beef, this road does not lead to Alexandra,' his mother said.

'You want a licence, right? So are you going to argue with the instructor?' he demanded. 'Turn right, turn right, straight on, left...'

Rakgadi sheepishly followed directions, even though it was clear that they were not going anywhere near Alexandra.

'Stop!' Abuti Beef shouted as they came to a house, one in a maze of hundreds of similarly built houses. 'Who wants to come in with me?' asked Beef. Only Ausi Nono volunteered.

Inside, the table was laid in a manner that indicated that an important visitor was expected. Ausi Nono was simply introduced as 'my younger sister' without being told who the host was.

The penny dropped. Ausi Nono realised this was the home of Abuti Beef's girlfriend and he had been grumpy because his plans for a romantic rendezvous had been messed up. But Ausi Nono was not complaining. The unnamed girlfriend turned out to be quite a chef and served one of the best lunches she had ever eaten.

As I said, my granddad took no nonsense from anyone, and as king of his empire, he made rules that no one dared break. One Friday evening, after Abuti Beef had left school and started working, he knocked on the window of the 'big house' – my granddad's grand house. Over weekends, it was full of his many grandchildren.

'Beef, why are you knocking on the window? Why don't you come in?' the old man called to his grandson.

'Mahayana (no one knows why Abuti Beef gave my granddad this nickname), what time is it?' he asked Ou 4 (another of my grandfather's nicknames). The latter referred to the location of the house, on 4th Avenue in Alexandra.

'Five past nine,' Ou 4 called back in his raspy voice.

'Right. You said no one may come into your house after nine o'clock. So I'm not coming in,' Abuti Beef told my grandfather.

What followed was a demonstration of the *chutzpah* [cheek] that made Abuti Beef the darling of the family. He called Ausi Nono to the window and handed her his rent money (once you started working and lived on my granddad's property, you paid rent). Ausi Dipuo was then asked to come to the window to get his weekly bus fare and keep it for him. Ausi Manki was called to collect money for my granny, which was Beef's contribution to the household groceries. Ausi Sthandi's role was to pick up his dry cleaning and she too made the trip to the window to get the money. Ausi Nono was called to the window again to get some small change that the girls would share among themselves. As they traipsed backwards and forwards from the window, Ou 4 was screaming blue murder, but he didn't stop the traffic.

'Why didn't Abuti Beef just call one of you and give you everything,' I once asked Ausi Nono.

'That would have been out of character,' she said.

Papa Blackie

Black men don't cry. That was the mantra by which black males were supposed to live. To make sure that this was well understood, my old man, Chum (the nickname he acquired by calling everyone, male or female, 'chum'), made sure that he beat the hell out of you when you cried – while telling you to shut up. Everyone, that is, except Papa Blackie. My dad had three brothers – and his fourth, unofficial brother was Papa Blackie. They were inseparable as they grew up together, raised on adjoining streets. But they went their separate ways when Chum went to teachers' college and spent time in other parts of the country.

Legend has it that, by virtue of their similar builds, when each set of parents bought clothes, they bought for two. And when they offended or angered my grandfather, they went to sleep at Papa Blackie's – and vice versa. Unfortunately, when the message was relayed about where they were spending the night, the hosting father got to know that the reason was mischief, and they got it on their bums.

As luck would have it, when the forced resettlement from Alexandra Township to Diepkloof took place, Wally – that was how Papa Blackie always referred to Chum – and Papa Blackie ended up living two streets apart. Papa Blackie was as much a fixture of the Molete household as his friend Wally.

I have never heard the two exchange a friendly word. But with one or two beers in their bellies, especially on Saturday evenings, the two could belt out a song or two. 'Mona Lisa' was their favourite, and you could hear them from the corner, six houses away, singing at the top of their voices, Uncle Wales with his tenor, and Papa Blackie a deep baritone. To this day, I only know the first line of the song, because that is all they sang, arm in arm, those Saturday nights.

Uncle Wales had a way of embarrassing us. Whenever we made him angry for one or other reason, he would clean the front *stoep* in full view of passers-by. Our friends always ragged us for making our father work! One Saturday morning Papa Blackie found Uncle Wales up to his embarrassing tricks.

'Wally,' he shouted across the street, 'why are you doing women's work?'

'Blackie, don't come in here.'

'*Thlogo ya rrago* [Your father's head – Papa Blackie's favourite curse], *ke tlo tsena* [I will enter].'

As Papa Blackie neared the gate, they repeated their threats and counter-threats. Uncle Wales moved to the gate to stop Papa Blackie from entering.

Imagine two giants, both strong of limb and around six feet tall, shoving each other around. Nothing much was said in this encounter until Papa Blackie retreated with the words: 'Wally, *thlogo ya rrago*, you will never see me at your house again.'

'Go to hell,' was my father's response. We thought that this was it; one of the longest-running friendships was over. That evening, the strains of 'Mona Lisa' coming from the street was the most reassuring sound we had ever heard.

If there was a weakness in Papa Blackie's heart, it was his inability to share his alcohol with anyone else but Uncle Wales. When he was broke, he would invoke the Tswana idiom *motho ke motho ka batho ba bang* [you are who you are through others]. Yet, when he had something in the kitty, he would deflect requests for sharing by intoning another Tswana idiom, *Mphemphe ea tshwenya, motho o kgona ke sa gagwe* [it is preferable to have your own than to ask of others].

This made a lot of their friends fume, as happened at one of Uncle Wales's family gatherings. While Uncle Wales and Papa Blackie were having their millionth argument to date, Papa Sam, one of their drinking mates, pleaded with Uncle Wales to join him in *bliksemming* [beating up] Papa Blackie.

'Blackie, did you hear that?' Uncle Wales responded. 'He wants me to fight you, my brother.'

16

'*Thlogo ya rragwe*,' Papa Blackie responded.

Poor Papa Sam, he was verbally torn apart by this twosome. In less than ten minutes, he was gone.

At another of my old man's *stokvels*, a pale Mama Grace, one of the guests, told my mum and Mama Betty, Papa Blackie's wife, to intervene before the two killed each other as they were arguing ferociously. 'Oh, let them,' Mama Betty and my mother answered in unison.

When the news came that Papa Blackie had died, Uncle Wales cried. It was the first time I saw a black man cry.

The concert

If ever an inquest were held into my love of music and my inability to learn the lyrics, my old man would have to be held accountable.

An accomplished organist with the tenderest of tenor voices, he sang in the choirs of all the schools he attended. He also taught music during his short teaching career. My granddad had bought an organ for his family, which my dad inherited. The organ ended up in our stove as fuel, as there was no space for it in our four-roomed house, shared at that time by seven souls.

I don't recall Papa ever singing a song from start to finish. He suffered 'choral interruptus', one might say. To be sure, most of the singing was inspired by whatever alcoholic drink he had indulged in that day. And if he was with best friend, Papa Blackie, it got frustratingly worse. They would start a song, and midway through 'Moon River' one of them would screech, 'Remember this one. Those were the days.'

'Yes chum. Not this rubbish *wahwahwah doomdoomdoom* they play on radio these days,' his friend agreed.

My mother was no slouch either. She had a sweet voice and, when the mood moved her, would join in. And then she would express her frustration when they interrupted their singing with their reminiscing.

When I was eight or nine years old, we had visitors one evening. My father's older brother, Tosa, brought his three daughters, Snaky, Stlankie and Mankoko, over to our house. A rare visit and, considering that it was in the middle of the week, very special. It was one of the girls' birthdays, probably Snaky's, and they brought with them a consignment of party goodies: cakes, cool drink and sweets, enough to feed the eight children there, three times over.

After Uncle Tosa left, the party really got going. We had a small, battery-operated radio – FM we called it in those days – and after singing 'Happy Birthday' to the birthday girl, the FM proved inadequate for our musical needs. We decided to hold a concert, right there in that small kitchen. As I recall, it started with Sunday school choruses and graduated to wedding songs. We sang solos, formed quartets, trios and everything in between and beyond. 'Tswang, tswang', 'Thelledi, thelledi', 'Mmangwane nthekele serantabole', 'Ba ile ba nake'; all got thrown into the mix as we sang and danced. And then my dad taught us 'There was a Gincigonco', which he said he had learnt in Natal.

Gincigonco is a verbal representation of a

seesaw as it goes up and down. When it is sung, two groups stand opposite each other and each sings the alternate lines of the song. One group goes up and the opposite side goes down, moving from the knees, resembling the movement of the seesaw. This song is probably the only one that I can sing in its entirety. The song goes:

Verse 1
There was a *gincigonco*,
There was a *gincigonco*,
There was a *gincigonco*, *gincigonco*, *gincigonco*,
gincigonco,
There was a *gincigonco*,
There was a *gincigonco*,
There was a *gincigonco*, *gincigonco*, *gincigonco*,
gincigonco.

Verse 2
There was a *gincigonco*,
There was a *gincigonco*,
There was a *gincigonco*, *gincigonco*, *gincigonco*,
gincigonco,
There was a *gincigonco*,
There was a *gincigonco*,
There was a *gincigonco*, *gincigonco*, *gincigonco*,
gincigonco.

Verse 3
There was a *gincigonco*,
There was a *gincigonco*,
There was a *gincigonco*, *gincigonco*, *gincigonco*,

gincigonco,
There was a *gincigonco,*
There was a *gincigonco,*
There was a *gincigonco, gincigonco, gincigonco,*
gincigonco.

It was the best concert I have ever attended.

School

Jakes

Ah, the joys of summer – the time when we take advantage of our great weather to enjoy loud music, the usual charred meat, salads and copious amounts of alcohol. Apartheid ensured that there very few places of entertainment for black people. The Zoo Lake in Johannesburg became one of the few venues where the darkies could go at that time to let off some steam.

To ease into the pre-Christmas holidays and to bid each other farewell at the end of the school year, our class organised an annual outing to the lake where we would spend the day eating and dancing. As money was tight, we started putting money into the kitty after the June exams. A classmate who was more affluent than the rest of us was chosen as the banker. The idea was that each one of us would pay a stipulated amount into the fund so that come year-end, we would have enough money to buy food and (non-alcoholic) drinks. The intention was to ensure that even the poorest in the class would be able to join the whole class at the year-end *gumba* [party].

The only thing the indigent among us would then have to worry about was the R2 round-trip fare. That is how tight things were.

We used four buses on such an occasion: one from the *kassie* [township] to the city, then one from town to Zoo Lake, and the same two on the return journey. And this was what led Jakes to take advantage of us. A rogue of note, he was well liked but mistrusted by all. His mother worked as a seamstress at 'a factory' (the general name for the many clothing factories that employed black women for a pittance). She supplemented the family income by doing mending jobs at home for friends and neighbours.

One customer was Bricks, Jakes's classmate and closest friend. Bricks had handed his torn trousers to Jakes's mother for mending. Typical of Jakes, he ran out of clean school clothes and ended up coming to school in Bricks's pants, which fitted, one must add, dangerously tight around Jakes's fat bum. A heated argument ensued. Jakes, face grim and sounding very convincing, pointed out to Bricks that the pants he had handed to Jakes's mother were torn at the back, while the ones Jakes was wearing were slit around the knees, and therefore couldn't possibly be Bricks's. The following day a smug Jakes stood in front of the class and announced that Bricks was a real *moegoe* [fool]. 'Yesterday I wore your pants and you believed me when I said they were mine.' It was not in Bricks's nature to fight, and despite our guffaws and mocking, he slunk behind his desk, embarrassed.

But I digress. The point about the picnic was that one had to struggle for the bus fare on the day. On the last outing we had, Jakes implored us to lend him R2 as he had only R5 on him and he would give the money back once we were at the lake as he intended buying ice-cream from the vendors there. We obliged, knowing that the bus drivers got very testy towards schoolchildren who forced them to change 'big money' (as we called the larger denominations). On the bus to the lake someone paid Jakes's fare. When we returned Jakes said he had been so engrossed in the partying that he had forgotten to buy the ice-cream and get the change for his fare. So another plan was made for him to get home. When we were in the last bus, Jakes interrupted the reminiscing and duly informed us that we had been had. 'I did not have any money!' Were it not for the adults in the bus, I swear we would have killed Jakes.

Poor Bricks, he became Jakes's victim on another occasion when the school went on an outing to the Rand Easter Show. Here, too, in order to save on expensive victuals, we formed pairs and shared resources. For his sins, Bricks ended up being paired off with Jakes. On the return trip, a rather solemn Jakes confronted Bricks: 'Where were you, I have been looking for you the whole day!'

Bricks, hungry and despondent, responded: 'Where were *you*? I am the one who has been searching for you. Where is the food?'

'Ah,' said Jakes, 'how could I walk the whole

27

day carrying food in my hands? I just couldn't resist finishing it off when I didn't find you. And I thought the reason you didn't come to me was that you were fixed up.'

I think it was tears that welled up in Bricks's eyes. A few good souls offered him their leftovers.

Arthur's shoes

Al's vanity provided ample opportunity for us to rattle his chain. One day he rocked up at our favourite drinking hole in a bright yellow jacket.

'Jeez Al, what are you doing man?' Joe started. 'We still value our sight, man. Why do you blind us so?'

'Joe, the only difference between you and me is that *ek het* class en *jy het nie* class *nie* [you have none],' was Al's comeback.

'Class. Ha! Not with a hand-me-down like that!'

'Jissus, Joe. *Jy ken hoeveel kos die ding?* [Jeez, Joe. Do you know how much this thing cost?]' We all knew where this was heading.

'*Ei, sit jy, en laat ons drin*k [Sit and let's drink],' we told Al.

His jacket prompted a discussion of past disasters we had all had with our wardrobes. '*Ei*, do you guys remember what Joe wore at his wedding. Joe, *waar het jy daai kostuum gekry?* [Where did you get that outfit?]' we asked, referring to the Coon Carnival-type suit

29

he wore for his wedding. He'd looked like a circus ringmaster. '*En jy het ga-perm* [And you had your hair permed].' We slapped our thighs in mirth as we recalled one very dolled-up Joe at his wedding.

Things like this never got Joe down. 'That was nothing,' he said, as he told us about the oversized shoes he used to wear at school. 'They were hand-me-downs from my brother. I filled them with paper so that they didn't slip off too often. And if they were any colour but black, I would have them dyed,' he said.

'Ah, that's *fokkol* [nothing],' I said. 'I lost a new pair of shoes once and my dad, who only bought us one pair a year, said I should "see to finish". So for the whole of that year I wore the previous year's pair, which pinched like hell. I think that was the beginning of my corns.' Monty Python would have liked this.

Arthur took a long sip from his glass. '*Julle dink* [You think] you had problems,' he said. 'I went through my entire school career walking to school barefoot.'

'Hee, what happened?' we asked eagerly, hoping that this was one of Arthur's famed fairytales.

'My dad had bought a pair of school shoes for my sister Zen. As you recall, we played no part in what was bought for us. He asked Zen to try the shoes on. They were too small for her.' Needlessly, he reminded us of the dilemma faced by our parents in those days. No one dared to return damaged or unwanted goods as traders treated them like dirt when they tried to rectify any errors that may have occurred. 'I thought he was going to ask Zen if she had any friends whose parents would have wanted to buy the pair,' Arthur said. 'But he looked at me. "*Hei mfana, faka le qatholo* [Boy, wear these shoes]," he told me. I gave him a look that said "no ways". He shot back a look that meant either fists or the belt. And to be beaten, for what? Shoes? I decided to humour him. "Those shoes fit me like a glove!"'

'And then?' we asked.

'My dad told me calmly, "*Ezakho* [They are yours]", and walked to his bedroom.

'*Ei* sonny,' we sympathised between guffaws.

'My dad was the last to leave the house every morning and made sure I wore those damn shoes. I looked like a nurse in them. So I wore them to the end of the street each day and then dropped them into my rucksack. I made sure I got out of the house slightly earlier than my schoolmates in my street so that none of them would see me in those shoes. After about a month I threw the damn things away in someone's rubbish and told my dad they had been stolen while we were playing soccer.'

'So what did your father do to you?' we asked.

'He beat the crap out of me. But it was worth it.'

The teachers

'Modiboho, how can a donkey pray?' teacher Mankweng asked Ntate Modiboho. Our neighbours were having an argument about churches and the teacher had asked the preacher which church he attended.

Modiboho, a lay preacher at the Bantu Methodist Church, known as 'Donkey', had proudly proclaimed: '*Tonki e e senang molato* [The guiltless donkey].' The donkey in question was the one on which Jesus rode in the Bible.

Teacher Mankweng's penchant for quirky answers made him popular. He once asked his class a question, and when no one came up with an answer he told the class: 'If you don't know something, please ask.'

'Who should we ask, sir?' someone said.

'*Nkgono wa hao* [Your grandma],' he replied.

One person who will never forget Mankweng is Jabu. The following is a verbatim exchange between the two.

'John Dikapeso, where were you yesterday?' Mankweng asked Jabu.

'I was off sick, sir,' answered Jabu.

'What happened to you?'

'I was bitten by a dog.'

'Where did it bite you?'

'On my hand, sir.'

'*Simolla* [Start again].'

'Yesterday I could not come to school, because I was bitten by a dog. It bit me on the hand.'

'Where were you going?'

'To the shops, sir.'

'*Simolla.*'

'Yesterday I could not come to school, because I was bitten by a dog. It bit me on the hand. I was on my way to the shops.'

'What were you going to buy?'

'Bread, sir.'

'*Simolla.*'

'Yesterday I could not come to school, because I was bitten by a dog. It bit me on the hand. I was on my way to the shops. I was going to buy bread.'

'White or brown bread?'

Out of frustration, Jabu began to cry.

As quirky as Mankweng was, we liked him. One rogue teacher was 'The Horse', whose claim to fame was that he inflicted more pain on us than any other teacher in the school. 'I will hit the neck, and the neck will tell the brain, 'Hey man, work, we are suffering,' was always his prelude to a beating.

He was also our athletics master. He'd run us into the ground, and if we complained of exhaustion, his standard response was: 'Tired? Tired? Ah, you're not dead yet, so run.' For some inexplicable reason, no one really hated 'The Horse'; he was a lovable character despite his cruel streak.

Our two favourite teachers were Kati, who taught us Biblical Studies, and Meneer, who taught us Afrikaans. Kati peppered his lessons with incredible anecdotes. Teaching the tale of Jacob and Esau, he said the reason Esau had lost out on his inheritance was that he did not put atchaar in his father's food! Each time the bell rang to signal an end to Kati's lesson he would terminate his class, pronto, even if he was in the middle of one of his funny stories.

'Ah, Meneer' we would groan in protest.

'*Bana ba me, ha ke patellwe* overtime [My dear children, I am not paid overtime],' he would say, clearing his things away.

Similarly, Meneer, a lovable old sage, aware that Afrikaans was not a subject particularly well liked by our generation, did his best to make us appreciate the 'language of the oppressor'. One way of doing this was to tell us about our predecessors' essays, which had us rolling in mirth at our desks. His favourite was one by a Cecilia, who had written about a sports meeting she had attended. 'Man, this was one of the best essays I have ever come across. No mistakes. Neat handwriting. Perfect Afrikaans. But I was bothered by one non-Afrikaans word. Cecilia said that when their team won, they had all shouted: '*Hadibajee!*"

Meneer rattled off a long list of Afrikaans reference works that he'd consulted to try to find an Afrikaans pronunciation of the word. He gave the class their essays back but told Cecilia that he was withholding hers as he was still trying to clarify something in it. 'After a week of consulting far and wide, I asked Cecilia to come and explain this word to me. She stood in front of the class and screamed: "*Ha di ba je!*"' We rolled in our desks. This was a Sotho encouragement to warriors in war and players in games!

Our music teacher, Londy, was a lovable tyrant as well. He portrayed himself as a tough guy and, despite the fact that he beat the living daylights out of us now and then, he mixed well with the pupils. Mike and Jeff were regular Londy victims. Mike was as black as darkness and we called him 'Satan' – behind his back, of course. He knew of his nickname, though. Sometimes during break when lots of school children were in the yard, Londy would call out to Mike: 'Hey Satan, come here.' Invariably Mike would not respond. 'Mike, I am calling you,' Londy would shout again.

Mike would make his way to Londy and tell him, 'Meneer, I don't like that name.'

Londy would proffer an apology and send Mike on a nebulous assignment like going to tell another teacher that 'the after-school meeting is still on'. As soon as Mike was some distance away, Londy would shout for our entertainment, 'Hey, Satan, tell him also not to forget his jacket!

As for poor Jeff, tone-deaf as he was, he got

roped in to Londy's choir every year at choir competition time. Then, on the Friday before the contest, he would get ditched. One year, cruel Londy ditched him on the Saturday morning of the competition. Particularly galling was the fact that he had had to borrow the school blazer to perform in the choir that morning. When Londy assembled his choir the following year, Jeff questioned his inclusion, given the fact that he had never made it into the hall as a competitor. 'So you know music better than I do?' Londy asked him in a threatening voice. Jeff simply had to resign himself to his fate.

Then there was our Maths teacher, Simango, a Jim-comes-to-Jo'burg character who came to the big city and thought he was a hit there. He irritated the hell out of everyone by talking in the patois, wrongly pronouncing words in the lingo. We soon discovered his Achilles heel. Despite his attempt at flamboyance, he didn't prepare adequately for his lessons. As our maths teacher, he gave us lots of homework. And when it was time to present our answers, he would stand at the blackboard as we shouted out our solutions to him. And that is how we discovered that he didn't prepare adequately. When there was a difficult problem and we didn't have an answer, he turned his back on the class and quickly worked out the problem on the board.

One day, when dealing with one particularly difficult problem, we decided that we wouldn't cooperate with Simango. No one shouted out solutions. Once he realised we were not buying his rubbish anymore, the plan was for one of us to stand up and tell him we knew that he didn't prepare for his lessons. Then the whole class would shout him down and cause a mini-riot.

'$2x$ by $4y$ is...' Simango waited for an answer.

'Eh, Meneer, you don't prepare,' I offered by way of taking the matter forward.

'What?'

'You don't prepare, Meneer,' I repeated.

A model pupil, I had never been chastised by a teacher before. Simango laid into me and gave me a full dressing-down. At one stage I even thought he was going to beat the hell out of me. There was not a squeak from my classmates. To this day, I refrain from doing things with groups. I refuse even to belong to a *stokvel*.

Hit the skakava

The problem with learning many languages is that it takes time to perfect the new medium. The consequences can be hilarious. And believe me, English is a difficult language to learn, especially when it is taught, as it was to us, through our indigenous languages. Just after our country became part of the civilised world in 1994 and the national airline started hiring black crew members, a story is told of an Englishman, on a flight from London, asking a black air hostess for 'black pepper'. She promptly brought him a copy of the *Sowetan*, the black-owned newspaper.

At a time when Otis Redding's 'I've Got Dreams' was a popular hit, my kid sister entertained us with the following words from the song: 'I got dreams, I got dreams, to Miranda.' The right words are: 'I've got dreams to remember.'

One of the major criticisms of the Bantu education system was the way we were taught – by rote. We had to repeat things and scream out the answers. On one occasion our English teacher was getting us to learn words ending with 'hood'. The 'motherhoods', 'fatherhoods' and 'sisterhoods' came flooding in from all corners of the class. Mzala, not the most stupid chap in class, stopped us in our tracks when, asked for his contribution, he answered: 'Firewood.'

And then there is the problem of not knowing what is slang and what proper English. I was behind a client in a bank queue when I heard him tell the clerk: 'This card is fucked up.' Poor girl, she reddened with either anger or embarrassment. I intervened and explained that where we came from, 'fucked up' is a normal expression for 'damaged'.

An accused in court once testified: 'I was with my friends walking two-two with our four-fives and when we stopped for a six-nine these guys demanded tigers. Nine nine, just like that your honour.' The interpreter translated: 'We were walking in pairs with our girlfriends when we stopped to pee and these guys accosted us demanding money. Just like that, your honour.'

The (white) magistrate to the interpreter: 'Mr Makhubela, there were a lot of numbers there. You did not repeat a single one of them in your translation.'

Makhubela: 'Your Honour, my translation was absolutely perfect. That's the *tsotsi taal* used in the townships.

Back in the classroom, the science teacher once asked, 'Suppose air was water, what would happen? Yes, Pule?'

An enthusiastic Pule answered, 'We would hit

the *skakava*.' Hitting the *skakava* was our term for swimming.

Community

Pick Six

Name a horse, and more often than not Pick Six would rattle off its lineage. He knew the pedigree of each horse. When he faltered, he said it was because the horse was 'new' or 'useless'. Horse racing was Pick Six's life. He pored over every racing booklet he could lay his hands on, reading about horses' past performances, the stables they came from, their trainers, jockeys. He was a walking encyclopaedia on the sport of kings. He ingratiated himself with one or two jockeys and stable hands, getting 'hot tips' that added a few bob to his winnings.

'Don't worry,' he reacted when people said he was wasting his money on the nags. 'One day, I am going to hit the big one. When I hit the Pick Six, don't come rushing to me for money.' And that is why he was called Pick Six. So in love was he with the name that when you called him by his name, Benjamin, he quickly corrected you: '*Ke* Pick Six, *ntate*. Pick Six.'

He picked a winner now and then. Enough to ward off his wife Mapule's complaints: '*Hei wena* [hey you], that dress you wore to your cousin's wedding was bought with my winnings. What about the dining-room suite? I paid spot cash for it. So, *ska ntena* [don't bug me].'

'But Ben,' wailed Mapule, 'if you had saved all the money you've fed to the horses, we could be living in Sandton by now.'

'Don't worry, baby. When I hit the big Pick Six, you will have a mansion in Houghton. Your mother can live downstairs.' And so it went.

When casinos were introduced in the country, Pick Six tried his hand at gambling. 'Boring. Boring,' said Pick Six after a trip to the casino. 'These machines have no life. Someone doctors them so that you cannot win easily. With horses, you study the form and hit the jackpot.'

'Ben, what do you want to do with our lives? You can't go on like this. At least invest in an insurance policy,' Mapule once pleaded with him.

'No, no insurance. I buy insurance; you kill me. I know you women. Look at Molefe. The poor guy is dead and his wife is driving flashy cars bought with his insurance money. And every young boy in the township is now crawling under her skirt. Forget it. I belong to a burial society and, if I die, there will be a decent funeral. We will be rich one day, believe me, baby.'

When the lottery was introduced, it suited Pick Six to a T. 'You choose six numbers and you win five million bucks. This is better than horses. *Tata ma chance, tata ma millions* [Take a chance, win millions],' he enthused, echoing the advertising slogan of the lottery. He started buying all the gimmicks clever marketers put out after the introduction of the lottery: dream books, random number pickers, and for the first time he started buying the newspaper on Fridays so he could check out the column about 'all the winning numbers so far'. The rest of the newspaper went into the trash bin.

Still, as with horses, he missed by the odd two or three numbers and his pickings were meagre indeed. But he kept his faith in the numbers and awaited his big day. In fact, last weekend he hit the big number. All six of his numbers popped out of the Lotto machine and the prize this time around was a cool million smackeroos. On Monday, when he went to collect his winnings, he was paid out R2.50: there had been two million winning tickets. He had spent R50. 'To hell with this thing. I am going back to the horses,' Pick Six said.

Rambo

Rambo was not the sort of person taken to measured, rational behaviour, which is how he got his nickname. Those who knew a bit about him told of his explosive temperament. His temper was connected to a short fuse that did not even need to be lit. Some erudite clown once said he had a rambunctious nature. The phrase caught on. But, due to the difficulty of the native tongue in pronouncing 'rambunctious', and the creativity in issuing nicknames, he ended up with the label 'Rambo'.

The occasion was a party at which liquor was in good supply, and jokes – more like insults when sensitivities are dulled by the abundant alcohol – were also in good supply. Someone, probably Sbo, the village clown, cracked a joke about the shape of Rambo's head, a structure so conical that everyone had an opinion on it, but no one who was sober would dare to express it. Needless to say, Sbo's remarks did not go down well with the object of ridicule. A warning was issued. But oiled by the laughter and the juices of the vine,

Sbo threw in a rejoinder. The reprisal was swift. A bottle of brandy landed flush on Sbo's head. Shards of glass littered his head. Warm alcohol glazed his face. He was saved by the baseball cap he wore, and the fact that he had closed his eyes at the moment of impact. As the group around them separated the two, Rambo retreated, issuing an ominous warning: 'Next time I will cut your balls off.'

Those who grew up with him blamed Rambo's head for his nature. Growing up among township boys who held nothing sacred, he was always the butt of cruel jokes. The teachers he complained to, instead of muttering reassuring words, also called him names linked to the shape of his head. His parents were not much help either – his mother an incorrigible drunk, and his father a sorry cuckold. In short, they had their problems and Rambo featured very far down on their list of priorities. Having built him his own room in their backyard, they judiciously avoided him unless it became imperative. So by and large he had to fend for himself in the way of the townships – by beating the hell out of anyone who dared cross his path.

Despite this, he had a series of nicknames, mostly whispered behind his back. In time 'Rambo' stuck and no one even remembered his original name. Ask anyone to tell you what it was, and they were likely to give you one from the series of nicknames that had adorned his life. But he was not a bully – far from it. His own description of himself was that he took no shit from anyone. In his own words: 'You give me shit, I give you two.' For a while, 'Two-shits' was added to the list of his nicknames. He had no one that he really could call a friend. He joined in at any social gathering that presented itself; a funeral here, a wedding there, a party, a *stokvel*. No one really minded or asked questions – until they had the bad judgment to make a remark against him in his presence, that is.

As for girlfriends, he made do with any drunken tart he could lay his hands on. And frankly, in a township were alcoholism was seen more as the norm than an aberration, sex was the least of his problems. He regarded the occasional visit to the clinic for treatment of some venereal disease as a trophy of his manhood. Even the nurses gave up imploring him to use condoms.

No one knew where Rambo worked. He took the bus in the morning and returned in the evening like everyone else. When asked where he worked, his curt response was 'in town'. In December he took leave like everyone else. And then Rambo died. He was found naked and prostrate on his bed. The door was ajar, which is what forced his mother to peep in. With so many people dying in the township each day, the police did not bother with a proper post-mortem or investigation. The death certificate stated that he died of 'natural causes'. But the tongues in the township knew better. Some say that when he left the shebeen that evening, he was so drunk he died of alcohol poisoning. Others said they saw him leave with a woman and she killed him. No one knows which for certain.

The village idiot

Every village, in this case township, has one – a village idiot. This is the character that mothers use as the bogeyman and the children in the street make fun of. In many cases they are illiterate characters. In others they are what is now loosely called mentally ill. Or they fall somewhere in between.

As a child growing up in the ghetto, in an environment where the only illness that we cared about was physical, other types of sicknesses were perceived either as bewitchment, irrationality or sources of amusement. In hindsight – and perhaps with enlightenment – I realise that the following incidents should never have happened. Alas, they did, and I am not sharing them as an act of voyeurism, but as part and parcel of the sharing that has taken place elsewhere in this book.

Washo lived in the same street as my grandparents, and my encounters with him were during the school holidays when we were shipped off to visit grandma and grandpa. Given that the last of this pair left this earth when I was eleven years old, my encounters with Washo took place early on and were few, though still vivid. No one knew where he came from. He worked for a very popular shebeen queen, who, it must be said, looked after him well. When he died, she gave him a dignified farewell. He was quite a mild character and always in a rush as he performed chores for the shebeen queen. But each time we kids called out to him 'Washo!' he would stop and reply, 'Wash your bloomer, because dirty!' That is how he got his name.

And then there was Mmutlanyane (little rabbit), who got his name because of the pack of greyhounds that he used for hunting rabbits in the fields on the outskirts of the township. Frankly, I don't recall ever seeing him with a catch. He, too, lived in the same township as my grandparents. We really riled Mmutlanyane when we called out to him: 'Mmutlanyane, *bula motete, moya o kene* [Open your bum so that it can get some air]!' At best, he swore at us. (As you are going to share this story with your children, I don't think it would do me any favours to repeat Mmutlanyane's peppery language here.) At worst, he would threaten to set his dogs on us.

One particular school vacation, when it seemed everyone had visited their grandparents, we played our usual trick on Mmutlanyane. Perhaps it was the fact that we were so many that made Mmutlanyane chase us. We scrambled all over. We – my siblings and the myriad cousins that had visited our grandparents – ran into the house.

Being a large house, it was easy to hide: under tables, behind cupboards and in other rooms. For some crazy reason Mmutlanyane decided to concentrate on the Molete clan. Alone in the house was my Granny, the most angelic grandma anyone can wish for. Mild-mannered and hard of hearing, she was reposing in her favourite chair, probably eating fruit and humming a hymn. That is what she did most of the time, but with Mmutlanyane in pursuit, taking in every detail of what Grandma was up to was a luxury none of us could afford at that time.

The tragi-comedy that followed saved us. We were all within earshot when we heard him tell Granny: '*Bana bana ba nthohaka. Ba re ke bule sebono moya o kene* [These children are swearing at me. They say I must open my bum to let the air in].'

'*Wa reng ntata?* [What are you saying, sir?]' Granny asked.

'*Ke re: Bana bana ba nthohaka. Ba re ke bule sebono moya o kene!*' Mmutlanyane repeated with a slight irritation in his voice.

'*Wa reng ntata?*' Granny asked again.

A now rather incredulous Mmutlanyane screamed at my Granny: '*Nkgono* [Grandma], *ke re: Bana bana ba nthohaka. Ba re ke bule sebono moya o kene!*'

Incredibly, Grandma asked the same question one more time! I bet you, if Mmutlanyane were white, he would have been red in the face. He stormed out: '*Ache nkgono, o tshwana le bona bana bana*! [Hell Grandma, you are just like these children!]' Phew!

Nothing seems to change. Recently I was visiting my mother in Diepkloof, and just around the corner from her house I saw a group of children doing exactly what my street friends and I used to do decades ago. The youngest among this group was no older than six years old. They were having fun at the expense of some fellow, old enough to be their father, who was obviously not a hundred per cent upstairs. And it was obvious that this was a frequent occurrence. As he came too close to them, they shouted, '*Matha!* [Run!]' He ran a few paces. Then they said: '*Jumpa*! [Jump!]' and he jumped up and down for a few paces. Lastly they shouted, '*Tsipa!*' He performed a *tsipa*, a contemporary dance that entailed pressing your buttocks firmly together several times. They guffawed and he joined in the laughter.

But Pongo, though strictly speaking not an idiot, was much more fun. I met him three times in my life. The first time our youth club was travelling in a bus and Pongo was standing right at the front, facing the passengers. He sang: '*Ka tabola panty ka dibono*! [I tore the panty with my buttocks!]' Just that one line, over and over again. In between, he would pause and tell us how he was our father and he was the person who had piloted the aeroplane that brought us to earth. The next time I came across Pongo was a week before Christmas, again in the company of some youth club members. We had accompanied one member, who was Pongo's neighbour, to his home. We chorused our greetings to him. He lit his pipe, puffing a plume of smoke into the air: '*Bana ba ka, ka Keresemose ke batla le tle ha ka. Mme o tla le phehela custard le jelly.*' It was an invitation to a Christmas lunch where we would be fed jelly and custard. None of us took up the mad Pongo's offer.

Within a fortnight, while walking one of our friends home, we met Pongo again in the street. 'Ntate Pongo, do you still have the jelly and custard you promised?' one of us asked. '*Mosadi wa ka ha a phehe masepa ano* [My wife does not cook that shit],' was his rather irritated response.

Cousy

He was the most organised of us, all eighteen years of him. While our small clique of friends in the youth club all called each other Cousy, for some reason it became his *nom de guerre*. As he was so organised, any activities of the club that needed a committee fell on Cousy's shoulders. We became the main act, performing duties that he assigned to us. And when other youth clubs visited, it was not difficult to guess who would be in charge of catering. Even the girls took their cue from Cousy. '*Hei lona banyana, ganti ba le rutileng ko magalona? Ganti ga le itse go thlokomela baeng* [You girls, what were you taught at home? Aren't you able to look after your guests],' was Cousy's favourite admonition to the girls whenever he lorded it over the catering.

During ballroom dancing lessons, he took the role of either the male or the female dancer, depending on the needs of the instructor. He became more of a mentor and coach to the younger dancers, especially the females. And he was quite popular with them.

His fashion sense was a bit peculiar. He liked scarves – a sissyish quirk in our books, considering too that he was a bit on the fat side. So was his insistence on stuffing his trousers in his boots. '*Hoodoo, Cousy, ha le itsi* fashion [You know nothing about fashion],' was how he defended his dress sense. Despite this, we loved Cousy. He was also handy in another sense. Whenever we needed to interface with parents, he led the negotiations. His demeanour and humility made mothers especially feel at ease with him. As a result, if it was a trip we needed approval for, or extra help we needed for a function, when Cousy led the talks we got what we wanted.

And if his dress sense was *kak* [crap], so was his choice of girlfriend. He dated the ugliest, clumsiest girl in the club. The relationship was being 'run underground' and we would not have known about it were it not for the fact that Aggy fell pregnant and stopped coming to the club. '*Hoooo* Cousy,' he told us on Monday afternoon at the club. '*Maobane batsadi ba ga Aggy bane ba le ko gae ba re ke mo pregnentesitse. Mokwena o ba tlile a mpolaya* [Yesterday Aggy's parents came to tell mine that she is pregnant. Dad nearly killed me].' The resulting child was a combination of Aggy's ugliness and Cousy's pudginess.

Then disaster struck: June 16, 1976 – the day of the Soweto youth uprising – fell upon us. We were all victims of the uprising, having to stop school prematurely because of the constant riots. As schooling became impossible, especially for those in the last years of high school, many of us went looking for jobs. Cousy found work on the mines in Carletonville as an assistant cook. Many years later, Mzi, another club member, told us that he had met Cousy at Irene's shebeen in Orlando. '*Hoooo* Cousy,' was Cousy's greeting. '*Ke kereile monna* [I found a man].' Mzi ignored this. 'Cousy, *kana ka re ba nnja*,' he said, emphasising to Mzi that he was someone's girlfriend.

We should have known.

After high school

Ou Phil

'Guys, I have never been so pissed off in my life. My old man had had one too many and he lay sprawled at the bottom of the stairs. I think he gave up after taking one step and passed out. My mother was already upstairs and it was left to me to drag the old-timer up the stairs,' Phil told us.

Hell, we all had fathers who drank themselves merciless. All six of us in the room had a story to tell of how, on one or other occasion, we had had to leave our dads sleeping in drunken melancholy on the kitchen table, or had to help our beleaguered mothers drag them to their beds. As usual, Phil had to go one up on us. His dad had had to be dragged up the stairs.

'What you are really telling us, Phil, is that you guys live in a double-storey house? Not a miserable four-roomed rondavel like the rest of us,' said Pule.

'Aw, come on, guys. You know that. I have told you that before. You have been to my house, and you know that,' responded Phil in mock horror.

We were shooting the breeze in Mzi's room,

dreaming about the days away from 'varsity after yet another boycott-induced break. As usual, after each class boycott, legitimate or otherwise, we would congregate in someone's room following the enforced break, and share alcohol and exchange tales of our escapades. The usual stories were about the women we laid; the number of parties we went to; the fact that we were considered a necessary evil by our parents while at the same time we became their cheap indispensable labour – for some reason, each time we went home, there would be a room that needed painting, or an overgrown garden that needed attention.

Perhaps each of us exaggerated a bit. But Phil's embellishments put us on the correct side of righteousness. We called him *majiyane,* the liar. The reason was that his truth contained a lot of untruths. What riled us was that he took us for buffoons and when caught out, he squirmed and lied his way once again out of the tough spots. Take the occasion he told us that the last time he was home he went shopping in his father's Lamborghini. 'Fuck you, Phil, no one in his right mind who lives in Soweto would buy a Lamborghini. Worse still, trust you to drive it into town,' Gibs told him.

'Serious, gents. He did. And it took me seven minutes. Seven! To get to town.'

'Okay, show us pics,' we screamed in a chorus, 'Give us proof!'

'Nah, I didn't take any pictures. But come December holidays, you guys can visit me and see the car. Whoa, that thing moves.' Those who visited him during those holidays did get to see his dad's new car – a Mercedes-Benz. 'My father decided the Lamborghini was too flashy for Soweto. So he changed it for this one.' None of us dared to ask Mr Gumbi. Knowing Phil, it would have been a futile exercise anyway, as we all knew what a pathological liar he was. We wondered how, in his adult life, Phil was going to cope in his chosen vocation of human resource management, given his capacity for lying. The last I heard of him was that he was getting divorced. His wife, it turns out, calls him 'Phil Promises'. 'And I am the one who has fulfilled each one of his promises,' she tells whoever will give her the time of day.

All cats are grey in the dark

Cats, I must say, are not the most popular animals in my community. If you own one, woe betide it be black, as you'll be accused of all sorts of wrongdoings. Chief among these is witchcraft. And as you might well guess, this does not make for easy living among the community. Ironically, the word itself creates some of the most evocative images in the patois – albeit due to American influence. 'Cats' are said to be cool. Babes can be cats, too. But catfights can be nasty, bitchy affairs.

It was the nicer type of cat that reminded us of Alfie, the coolest cat in town. So cool was he, we always teased him about not melting in the summer. As with all cool cats, Alfie drew in the feline lot by the dozen. Sure, we were jealous; wouldn't you be? I mean, the man was a hit, and try as we might, we were always lacking. And even our sycophantic moves – dressing like he did, walking like him, talking like him, etc. – did nothing to give us an edge over the master of cool.

We put this down to the fact that his family was a bit better-off than ours, and were blessed with more than just ordinary looks. We lesser mortals were forced to try and work harder. But, as he got older, he started losing his touch. The older we got, the more ordinary his conquests became. Either that, or we lost our collective vanity. Dipuo, Beauty, Girlikie and Maggie looked more like our sisters than the magazine-cover girls that we had become used to seeing on Ali's side.

'*Wat gaan aan, auti?* [What's going on, buddy?] Are you dropping your standards?' we wanted to know.

'Gents, *phunda* is *phunda* [sex is sex]. I don't know why you are all so obsessed with what's up there, when we all know that what is important is what's down there,' Alfie said philosophically.

We could live with that. Until one fateful concert at the lake, when he was spotted with Sophie. Let's put it this way, even for those who believe that beauty is only skin deep, in the case of Sophie the skin was rhino thick. As one of us remarked: 'The body is passable, but the windscreen is something else.' At our next drink-up, we ragged Alfie over his latest nearest and dearest. 'Aaall-fie, how dark was it when you met Sophie?' 'You are brave, *broer*. To be seen with Godzilla's daughter in public!'

The brother was unfazed. 'Gents, gents. Don't you ever learn? How many times must I tell you that all cats are grey in the dark? Give me a beer.'

There were consenting nods all round.

Dumping the corpse

Whether you believe in the ecclesiastical definition of beauty or not, you would have to agree that the Manhattans' song 'Heaven must have lost an angel' did not do Matshediso justice.

Despite our obsession with western, or more specifically Caucasian, ideals of beauty, Matshediso did not fit them and, yet, all who crossed her path were left with a 'wow' afterglow. Her darkness, rather pitch-blackness, enhanced rather than diminished her beauty. Slightly short of what is assumed to be average height, she had a body that would do well fitted out in the skimpiest of bikinis, and would be just as captivating in the most expensive *haute couture* suit. Get two people to describe her beauty and you would end up with two extremes of exaltation about this symbol of African gorgeousness. Tebello, ever the one to coin a phrase, called her 'fantasma-gorgeous-grrreat-oooh'.

I remember the reaction the first time I brought her around to meet my folk – especially that of my big sister. '*Moleko, Sello. O motle tjee ena ke moleko fela* [With such a beautiful one you

66

are heading for trouble].' She also whispered something about beautiful women being lazy. Flushed with the success of a conquistador, I paid no attention to my sister. Of course, in the macho way that we like parading our paramours, she was a real catch, and for the duration of our liaison I was regarded as the 'main man'. My buddies' girlfriends hated Matshediso for always stealing the limelight whenever there was a get-together. Tough titties – their problem, not mine.

My sister turned out to be right. Beauty like this has its drawbacks – for the guys more than the women. Every Sipho, Mandla and Khensani who has a better public profile than mine, or drove a better car, or earned more than I did, did their damnedest to prise Matshediso from me. It sometimes led to childish arguments and, once or twice, at 'Sisi's tavern', almost to fisticuffs. Ironically, and contrary to popular belief, beautiful girls like Matshediso are Catholic in their monogamy. When I involved myself in arguments to protect our relationship, she threatened to leave me, because to her, this meant I doubted her loyalty. But then, confirming popular belief, Matshediso was not exactly what you would call an intellectual. Sure, she had a university degree and one or two diplomas. But that is as far as her brains went.

When asked to rearrange my wardrobe, she became genius personified. She matched my clothes in ways I never thought possible. For a while, I even relinquished the task of buying my gear to Tshidi-baby, as I affectionately called her.

And you can imagine the two of us in public – being my modest self, I can only say that we looked smashing. However, those private and public moments that required her to open her mouth beyond salutations were excruciating. If the topic was sport she confused players from different sports codes. She did not even keep track of players from her favourite soccer team, linking them to the club even after they had moved to greener pastures or, in one particularly embarrassing incident, had died. On politics and other general topics I always made sure that I disengaged us from the rest of the group and came up with some cock-and-bull private issue that I needed to discuss away from the group.

Luckily she was on top of the world regarding soapies and celebrity gossip, which made it quite safe to leave her in the company of other females. Try as I might to ram a bit of culture into her head, I was accused of not wanting to accept her as she was. Diplomacy, begging and bribery came to naught. Our relationship did not last long, actually. While I miss her and the adulation she brought me, I do not regret the break-up. Confessing to my close friend Billy about the termination, I told him that there were certain non-negotiables in a relationship. 'To put it simply, *bra*, I am tired of being a necrophiliac. I could take a brain-dead bimbo, but corpses are a definite no-no. And I tried, boss, I really did my best at resuscitation.'

'And you are not a doctor,' he mumbled sympathetically.

Pub crawlers

We were a rough bunch. It was not a roughness bred of violence. Ours came out of Friday nights that became *phuza* [party nights]. Come Friday night, barring a family disaster, we met at the drinking spot that was popular at the time. First it was the Ale and Hearty, a drinking hole opposite the Market Theatre that was the place of choice with the arty types. Famous for its draught beer, chips and great service, it was an affordable place for talking *kak* [crap] with friends until the wee hours of the morning.

There was a core group of six of us and, girlfriends or mistresses in tow, we would meet just about every Friday at The Ale. Our group would sometimes increase up to 20. Perhaps the most serious conversation we ever had was who would win the soccer derby the following day! As jokes flowed thick and fast, there never was a dull moment at our table. We did not have a reserved place, plonking ourselves down wherever we could. One famous night we were kicked out of The Ale for being too noisy!

When The Ale closed down, we moved to Ma-Hazel's. It was not the same and our sojourn there did not last long. Ironically, Ma-Hazel's was black-owned while The Ale's owners were white. Despite our avowed desire to support black enterprise as far as we could, the mood at Ma-Hazel's somehow did not meet our raucous needs.

For a while we flirted with Club Rio on Bree Street, owned by the Cohen brothers, famous for owning Fun Valley, a picnic spot south of Johannesburg. While it played great contemporary music, its major shortcoming was the fact that teenagers frequented it. We took leave of the place when, one Friday night, Mphakzo was bumped by one of them at the bar. When he pointed this fact out, he was curtly told by the twerp: '*Groot man, ke tla go vaisa blind* [I will beat the living daylights out of you].' This was a warning to Mphakzo that he would be given free reconstructive facial surgery.

We then discovered JJ's in Parktown. Not quite The Ale, but its happy hour, during which beer was sold at half-price, made it acceptable. The fact that we befriended Frontline, one of the waiters, made it an even more desirable proposition. Unbeknown to the owners, and against house rules, we bought beers by the dozen during happy hour. Frontline dutifully stowed these away for us, replenishing the supplies at our table as soon as we had cleared our orders. He knew who drank what and how many beers we would each pile away, and for that he got probably the fattest tip of all the waiters. Patronised largely by whites, JJ's hired a white musician whose white music made us drink even more. Probably the only person who appreciated his music was Frontline. The more we drank, the more he made in tips. Despite this much imbibing, there are very few nasty incidents worth recalling – as when JMM, after taking a girlfriend of many weeks home to Soweto, got lost on the way to his house. He only made it home four hours later.

In a similar vein, I famously went home, parked the car in the garage, left the garage door open and duly went to bed while the car was running. Thank God for wives, who never tire of reminding one of such things.

After JMM's funeral, a week after he died, we all went for a remembrance piss-up at JJ's. I have never drunk so much, and yet remained so sober. It was the last time the group ever met as a unit, or drank at JJ's.

Transport

The lack of wheels has never been an impediment in our quest for fun. Be it going to a concert or the theatre, or attending a party in the *kassie* [township] or any of the *kassies* where friends were living it up, getting there, by safe means or otherwise, was our primary consideration. As car ownership was a rarity in the townships, whoever had one, however decrepit, was king. If it could get us there and back, that was good enough.

A foretaste of things to come was provided at varsity in Alice when we wanted to attend a concert in East London, a distance of hundreds of kilometres. Being in the sticks, and returning to Johannesburg only during vacations, the lure of contemporary superstars in the neighbourhood was just too tempting. It was not only that. Varsity life for black students in the apartheid era was boring, as we had to attend institutions that were plonked in the middle of nowhere. Any excuse to get out was more than welcome.

The trip to the concert saw eight of us packed into Dlangezwa's Golf. This car legally accommodates five people – uncomfortably. A few of us in the car had normal-size bodies, but the rest were not going to win the Mr Slim Varsity body contest any time soon. To the discomfort add the fact that Dlengs drove 'spoon down' on the open road. 'Spoon down' means putting one's foot flat on the accelerator. '*Ngiyayivala* [I am going to put my foot flat],' he said between sips from the bottle of Ranger brandy being passed around. We could afford Ranger; it was the cheapest gut-rot available, good enough for students' pockets. We were really a source of pocket money for Dlengs on this occasion. We paid him for taking us to the concert, after which he returned, having some other business to attend to.

The return trip was a case of fortune favouring the brave. We stood on the main road, hitchhiking. Obviously, other than truck or minibus drivers, no one was going to stop to pick up seven rather unappetising young men who made all sorts of gestures to attract attention from passing motorists. Until Billy stopped. '*Waantoe*? [Where to?]' he asked.

'Aaaaliss! [Alice]'

'OK, Fort Hare. *Kom in* [Get in].'

The fact that we were one more than a volleyball team did not seem to bother him. We learnt that he lived in the nearby coloured township which we called 'Rooiville' (a play on the Soweto township of Rockville) and was on his way to visit relatives near Alice. 'Do you drink Ranger?' we offered.

'*Ek drink hom and ek dryf hom* [I drink it and

I drive it],' was his thirsty response, referring to his car, which shared the name of the alcoholic beverage. Mercifully, because of their quality, or lack of it, both are distant memories in the South African consumer market. If Dlengs's 'spoon' was disconcerting, Billy's was death-defying. At speeds nearing Formula 1 proportions, he would look over his shoulder when addressing his back-seat passengers. Someone in the front asked him if he was not afraid of knocking down goats, of which there were many along the trip. Billy's answer was hardly reassuring: '*Moenie worrie nie, ek stamp die bok dat die kak spat* [Don't worry, I will knock it until shit splashes all over the place].'

One evening, close to midnight, four of us were returning from a Phillip Tabane concert in Dube. Standing forlorn on the main road, we were contemplating a fifteen-kilometre walk to Diepkloof. Then a kind-hearted man stopped. His car was billowing smoke like a Sasol furnace. As soon as he opened a door for us, Tom told the man: '*E tswa musi* [It is smoking].'

'What?' he asked as though he didn't believe his ears.

'*E tswa musi*,' someone else confirmed.

'Oh, *e tswa musi*,' the driver repeated. 'Okay, *etswang ge* [get out].'

We trekked home.

An incident involving Tebza and his girlfriend illustrates the dangers we exposed ourselves to. After leaving a party around 4am with his girlfriend, they were accosted by a gang of about six men. Both ran away in different directions. Later that day, Tebza called on his girlfriend to find out how she had fared. 'So what happened to you?' she asked him.

'Baby, I had to run away. Under the circumstances, I had no choice,' Tebza said.

'*Le nna* under the circumstances, *ha ke sa go batla* [let's call the whole thing off],' and with that she terminated the relationship.

Jailbirds

Mercifully, I have never been a guest of the minister in charge of our jails. It therefore was intriguing to hear from some of the *groot manne* (the streetwise older guys in the township who had spent time in the chookie), who sing the praises of life behind bars. And while they were waxing lyrical, at home our parents warned us that spending time in jail was the most infernal of existences, the absolute sign that the individual had reached the sub-strata of human existence.

The only exceptions were made for people who had committed political crimes or misdemeanours. For instance, people sentenced for shoplifting were seen as some sort of heroes who were reclaiming from white business money that should have been paid to the workers, who were grossly underpaid. It was rammed into our heads that people who were in jail for 'trespassing', who broke the curfew when they found themselves without a dompas, or who had overstayed their allotted 72 hours in Johannesburg because they did not have the right stamp in their passes, were not criminals. In fact, it was their jailers who were so labelled, and the words 'those dogs' when referring to the police and officials of the justice system were frequently used in the Molete household, despite the ban on swearing in our house. (Until the 1960s, in some towns blacks were not allowed to be outdoors after a prescribed hour, and those who broke this curfew found themselves in the chookie.)

When topics turned to career ambitions, much as the old geezer did not want to choose for anyone, the civil service, including teaching, was not on the menu. My old man was one of the teachers who quit the profession in the 1950s when Bantu education became entrenched in law.

Among the people who glorified jail life was Papa Zee, a frequent visitor to many a jail for petty theft. As with all our neighbours (bar one household), he was a friend of our family and, as befitting our culture, a father figure. We were always allowed contact with him.

Each time he came out of prison – he seemed to go back every two years or so – he complained about the 'soft life' we boys led. On those occasions, whatever Papa Zee did was on the double. He always ran, or walked at a very brisk pace. He always washed in cold water, despite the season. '*Kom, kom, kom* [come, come, come],' is how he would get us to do anything. '*Julle laities is* soft [You youngsters are soft]. You need to spend some time in jail. Look how slow you are. Are you a woman, or what?'

Each time he came out of jail, his head was

clean-shaven and he had us spellbound, telling us how prisoners used broken bottles to shave each other's heads. '*En kyk*, not a scratch on my head. We know how to do any job thoroughly.' None of us bothered to find out how bottles were allowed into cells. One day, on our way to school, a group of workers were digging trenches to lay electrical cables. As the group went into a sonorous rendition of 'Shosholoza' when using their picks and shovels, Veiz, a recent graduate of Modderbee Prison, grabbed a pick from one of the men. What followed next was poetry in motion. Veiz lifted the pick, spinning it in mid-air and bringing it down swiftly. The movements were repeated rapidly – with the workers and passers-by standing there open-mouthed. Without a word, he returned the pick to applause and ululation from his audience. 'Timer, come to Modderbee and we will teach how to use a pick *en* shovel properly,' Veiz told the man he had taken the pick from.

But if ever there was anyone who thought prison was glory, it was Pankie, a goalkeeper in our senior soccer team. At least once a year, he made sure that he spent time in jail. He would commit silly crimes, such as urinating in public in view of the police, to get himself arrested.

'Bra Pankie, why do you like prison so much?' we wanted to know.

'Listen, where else do you get fed three meals a day without doing any work?' Pankie replied.

'But Bra Pankie, you could be getting even better food if you worked.'

'Listen, in prison there are no women, no one bugs you about anything.' This shut us up.

His favourite prison tale, which has become urban legend, was of a Mopedi man who, after being sentenced, was brought to Bra Pankie's communal cell. *'Thobela mapantiti* [Good day, jailbirds],' the Mopedi man greeted the group in the humble demeanour associated with his kinsmen. 'We *bliksemmed* him [beat him up],' Bra Pankie said.

Having being told how prisoners sadistically brutalised each other, no one wanted to know the gory details.

Ousies

There we were, dripping into our Friday night drinking hole, joining those who had arrived earlier, sharing the week's workplace misery. 'Molefe, *monna* [my man], come and join us,' we called out to a lonely figure caressing a bottle of beer. Usually a gregarious fellow, it was surprising to see him on his own.

'In a moment, gents. I've got a date with a new find and I don't want her to join you guys straight away. I want to bleed her into the group, you know?' was his reason for his solo stint. Knowing how rough the guys could get, we understood. Although our jokes sometimes bordered on the slanderous, regular members of the drinking circle never took much offence. But with neophytes, especially new girlfriends, it could be a different story altogether.

'Molefe,' Zakes called out thirty minutes later, 'Is she still coming?'

'She will be here now-now,' Molefe said, more to convince himself than us.

Another fifteen minutes passed and we screamed

at him to join us. He dragged his drink to the table. 'Molefe, how old are you?' Binto asked him.

'Thirty-one,' he responded.

'And at your age you still believe that if a woman does not pitch up within thirty minutes of the appointed time, she will pitch up at all?' Binto continued.

'But you guys don't understand. I called her on her cell just a few minutes ago and she said she was on her way. I could hear she was in a car,' Molefe defended his position.

'And how sure are you she was the driver? And if she was, whether she was driving this way?' Rich wanted to know.

'Those are the worst, my bra. The ones that sweet-talk their lies instead of lying straight out like their sisters,' Pule chipped in. 'Jack, you remember *daai een wa ko* [that one from] Meadowlands? *Daai ding was mooi maar sy was* real rubbish [she was beautiful but a right royal tart]. Each time *a batla ho ntshaisa krep* [she wanted to stand me up], she would say, "Haai honey, be patient *ke ya tla nou nou ne* [I will be with you in a moment]." Until one day I decided, to hell with this. I exchanged cars with another *bra van meine* [buddy of mine] and went to wait for her outside her home. And sure as hell, she was dropped off by another man. I waited a few seconds until they got into the house and then knocked on the door. Boy, her whole *blerry* [bloody] family was embarrassed,' Pule smiled triumphantly.

It was Pat's turn. 'Ousies, don't talk to me about them. I don't trust them. And I learnt my lesson when I was still in high school. Remember how we used to meet them in town?' One of the ways of meeting the ladies when we grew up was to accost the one who took your fancy when you were in town. With some verbal sparring, you would persuade your prospective to give you her name and address. 'You won't believe this. On two occasions I met different women who gave me their names and addresses,' Pat said. 'On the first occasion, I went to this place in Moletsane. There was a guy there who was gardening. I braved it and asked him if Ntombi lived there. He laughed. "*Ba kutholile* [You have been had]," he said. "I am the only child in this house!" We had a good laugh. But it was such a waste of time and money travelling all the way from Diepkloof just *go shaya krep* [to be stood up].'

Life went on and a year later Pat had another town encounter and was given an address in Moletsane. 'As I approached that house, it looked familiar. And guess what, it was the same house. I thought, well, maybe the old occupants have relocated and my new love lives there. When I knocked at the door, the same guy that opened the door for me a year earlier came out and recognised me. He laughed. "*Wena futhi. Ba zi tholele ngawe* [You again, you really have been had]." He bought me a cool drink and we shot some bull about how terrible women are.'

More beers were ordered. 'But the worst is

when they don't want you anymore. Why don't they just tell you to *fokoff* [go to hell] so you can start looking for someone better?' said Greg. 'I was once fired in the cruellest manner. I called Grace to arrange to go to movies. Her sister answered the phone. "Hi Tshepi, can I talk to Grace?"

"*Mang?* [Who?]" she asked.

"Grace," I repeated.

"*Hayi,* there is no Grace here. Wrong number." And she put down the phone.

'I called again. You know how self-doubt sets in and you say she is probably right about this wrong number thing.

"*Hau abuti* [sir], I told you, there is no Grace here." And she shouts at some other people: "*Hei bathong, gona le motho mo are o batla* Grace. *Le ea mo itse* [There is someone looking for a Grace. Do you know her?]" I could hear giggles in the background and I knew this was part of a well-planned plot to get rid of me.'

'And we still go looking for their sisters even when they break our hearts,' said Pule.

'Why, should we go for animals?' Greg asked.

The relief in Molefe's eyes was palpable: at least he was not the only one to have had such an experience.

Doleiksa

Contemporaries, in our case, did not always belong to the same age group. It was not unusual to find a ten-year-old among a group of five-year-olds. We called the older ones in the groups *ngotos* (someone older than their contemporaries but in the same company or group) as opposed to *groot manne* (big men). The latter is a recognition of someone much older and who was afforded some modicum of respect or fear. Even at school, each class had its *ngoto* – they were mostly males and in most cases these happened to be the dullest blokes in the room.

A story is told about one such *ngoto* who kept failing at school, thus being continually joined by younger and younger classmates. One day, when given an exercise to do, the *ngoto* tried to crib from his desk mate. When the latter protested, the *ngoto* apparently told him, with disdain in his voice: 'You think I care? At the end of the year the teacher is going to get rid of the whole lot of you and I will be the one that she loves and who will remain in her class.'

When bored of playing too much soccer or of fighting, we would find time to sit under one of the few trees in the *kassie* and shoot bull. Much mischief and daydreaming came out of these bonding sessions. It was under these circumstances that we tried our hand at smoking – even though at this stage we only smoked *dirwairwai* (dried leaves and seeds we picked from the veld close to where we lived) or *mosunpere* (dried horse dung). We practised speaking English – in reality gibberish that made sense only to us, for example: He you sonna-ofa-gun why you don't squank wit me?' We lied to each other about what we ate for supper and made ambitious plans about what we would be when we grew up. We formed a cappella group that sang only for itself.

And we chased girls. More appropriately, we bugged them. We taunted them about their looks, their clothes, and made suggestive remarks. The victims were the sisters of whoever was not with us at the time. The girl who attracted the most attention was Beulah. And the reason was her beauty. Had she been so inclined she would have been Miss Diepkloof, Miss Soweto, Miss School, Miss Church or even Miss South Africa. Unfortunately for South Africa, she was not so inclined, and the country has missed out on sharing one of the most engaging faces ever.

As we were engaged in a lot of nothing during one of these sessions, the girl of our dreams went past. 'Bulah!' Doleiksa, the *ngoto* by more than seven years, called out. We could never get

Doleiksa to pronounce her name right. '*Hei wena*, Bulah, come here!' he repeated.

'*Haai voetsek wena* Doleiksa. Who said I want you,' a sharp-tongued Beulah retorted.

Turning his attention to us, Doleiksa intoned: 'She does not know who I am. I will chase after her, catch her, *pomp* her *pomp* until she is pregnant; *pomp* her *pomp* her until she is bigger; *pomp* her *pomp* until she is this big, and then *pomp* her *pomp* until a child comes out!'

'Ya Doleiksa,' we concurred. 'Plus you are older than us, you can do a better job than the rest of us!'

Let's take it outside

Conflict resolution is not a strong point when you are young. Or, rather, negotiating a settlement is not. The only negotiating tools we grew up with were fists, catties (catapults) and, in extreme cases, knives. Our induction into this world started with the sand method. In primary school, someone in the group reporting that A had said something nasty about B would originate a fight.

'*He* sonny, did you hear what Piet said about you? He says you are a bed-wetter!'

'What does he know? Do I sleep with him?' And he also said, 'Your mother.' (Saying 'your mother' to someone may sound innocuous but it a great insult among black people.)

'*Wa mo tshaba*? [Are you afraid of him?]'

'What? His bum, man. I'll *blaas* him, he doesn't know who I am.'

In the meantime Piet was being told: 'Hey Piet, Mpho says your sister *ke sefebe* [is a bitch].'

'*Heee... O feba le yena* [Is she his whore]? His bum, man.'

'*Wa mo tshaba?*'

'No ways. Bring him here and I will kick him to kingdom come.'

The protagonists would be brought together. *'Hayi bambi, hayi tsipi, haai lome, hayi gwepi!* [No holding, no pinching, no biting and no scratching!]' we'd say as we formed a circle around them. Someone would scoop up two handfuls of sand. Whichever of the two tapped the hands of the sand-picker first would start the brawl. Piet and Mpho exchanged blows, while we encouraged them. They'd blast each other to smithereens and, when it was over, they would shake hands. No hard feelings.

During school holidays we would form soccer teams made up of guys from the same street or block and we would play against other teams. At least once during each holiday a fight would break out between the various teams. The ructions would be caused by a disputed occurrence: a foul, a penalty, corner kick, anything. Largely, these would be sorted out by swearing the pants off each other. There was always that one occasion when no amount of turning the air blue with expletives would bring a resolution. The immediate result was that fists and stones would start flying. If the dispute occurred early in the holidays, it would be a great inconvenience, as most of such fights lasted the entire holiday period. Individuals in the feuding camps would slug it out each time they met in the streets. And too bad if you lived at the lower end of the township and had to go through enemy territory when sent to the shops.

Our mothers were not in the least interested. You got sent to the shops and that was that. Running the gauntlet of taunts, fists or stones became one's life at this time. Come school again, all was over and forgotten until the next holidays.

Visiting male relatives our age also got roped into these fights. Of course, as we grew older the fights got fewer and fewer. *En nou die anne dag* [The other day] Thami told us of a sorry escapade. He was drinking at MamLady's with a bunch of friends. One reason why MamLady's was well patronised was Joyce, her daughter. Lithe of body and beautiful of face, she attracted leering lechers to her mother's joint like bees to the proverbial honey. Thami said each time Joyce came to take orders and clear the tables, a particular patron would jostle for Joyce's attention.

'I checked him out; he was so skinny that I knew that a quick one-two, one-two would put him in his place,' Thami, who is not quite a graduate of Weight Watchers, told us. *"Mfo, a si bonane nga phandle* [Buddy, can we see each other outside?]" I told him,' Thami continued. So out into the dark they went. *"Majita* [Gents] that guy had four hands. I could not parry him. I'd block his right and from nowhere I'd taste his left. Watching was Joyce, who kept telling us, *"No zo limazana"* [You will hurt each other]. And then he dropped me with a sledgehammer to my stomach and started kicking me on the ground. *"Onga ngikhahleli* [Don't kick me]," I told him. He stopped, and as soon as I was on my two feet, he resumed the punishment. Once satisfied, he let me be and joined the other drinkers in the house. I dusted myself off and joined the other guys. My lips were swollen, one eye was half-closed.' After settling down, the other guys, surprised at my condition, asked, "*Heyi mfo*? [Guy, what happened?" "*Hi le nja le* [It's this dog]," I lisped my answer, as I pointed to the stranger coolly sipping his beer.

Borotho

Uncle Matt was a driver all his working life. A delivery truck driver. 'And in all the places he worked,' Mama told us, 'his first delivery was to his house. Somehow, he managed to steal whatever merchandise his company was selling.' This is how we managed once to paint our house with automobile paint, after he had given it to his sister as a token of brotherly love. It took weeks before the darn thing dried! In township culture, what uncle Matt did is called getting *borotho* [bread].

This type of petty theft was not only condoned, but was also seen as an economic necessity – a means of augmenting the near-slave wages that many blacks were given. If anything, it was encouraged. And if you worked in a place where what could be stolen would be of use to many others in the neighbourhood, you were somehow expected to open a thriving business on the side. For instance, someone who worked in a stationery shop would make a killing when schools reopened in January.

Stories of how people sneaked goods out of shops are legendary. A fellow who worked in a butcher as a cleaner wore a rain suit under his overalls and wrapped boerewors all over his body, over the rain suit, before donning his overalls. Or else he packed the meat tightly in a plastic bag, dunked it into the bucket of water he used for cleaning floors, and each time he went to empty the bucket, a grateful recipient-buyer would be waiting for him on the pavement.

A classic tale is of the fellow who worked as a cleaner in a hardware shop. He used a wheelbarrow to get rid of the dirt. The security guard at the door always checked the wheelbarrow to see if any tools were concealed there. None were ever found. At the end of the financial year when the shop did a stock-take, they found thirty wheelbarrows missing, unaccounted for. The cleaner had already quit the company.

Furniture shops lose small items when the delivery crew conceal things such as irons or portable radios in fridges, wardrobes or freezers. I was in a taxi one day when two fellows who had not seen each other in aeons greeted each other thus.

'*Is jy die man? Lang tyd né?* [Long time no see.]'

'*Ja, lang tyd.* Do you still work at that place?'

'Yes.'

'And is it still in business?' the erstwhile co-worker asked with incredulity.

'No, *banna, ha le sebetse* [you guys are not doing much].'

It sparked animated discussions in the taxi. Just about everyone had a story to tell. Even the taxi-driver told us that he and his fellows do what is called *ukudontsa i-draada* [pulling the wire]. What happens is that taxi drivers have to cash in their daily takings with the owners every night. They have to hand in a set daily amount. Anything extra they pocket. But even if they did not meet the target, they still pocket some cash after lying about their takings. This system works to their advantage as taxis, unlike buses, do not use a ticket system.

One *ou toppie* [old man] showed how the *borotho* practice could be taken to extremes. 'You people don't know a thing. I work for one of those aeroplane places in Aeroton. My backyard is full of plane parts. Who the hell am I going to sell them to?' The mixture of pride and frustration was clear in his voice.

Maddock swears by this one. A chap who had lost many a job due to pilfering had to settle for a place in a mortuary out of desperation. One day he approached a family that was making funeral arrangements for their granny. '*Ha le ka mpha R50 nka le direla mokabelo* [If you give me R50 I will give something in return],' he told the family. (This is how workers made offers to shoppers, and if you fancied the offer, even if you did not know what item of merchandise would be coming your way, you would agree and whisper about meeting outside the shop to complete the transaction.)

The family of the bereaved, in muted tones,

told the chap where to stuff it. But he was persistent. A member of the family, fearing that if they did not make the payment, Granny's body might be desecrated, made the payment. 'On Friday evening, after the body was delivered to the house, they discovered what the R50 was for. Right at the bottom of the coffin, the chappie had left a perfect set of dentures – maybe for Granny to chew biltong in the next world,' Maddock said, gulping the last of his whisky.

Stadium

When you are young, and your hormones are running haywire, thoughts of rolling in the hay dominate your mind. Two challenges present themselves: catching the bird, so to speak, and finding the hay. The first, though achieved with much begging, cajoling, flattery and bribery, was relatively easy to attain. With tips from friends and one or two clandestinely obtained from a big brother, bagging the maiden was a cinch. To be sure, if you asked the direct question of an older brother about how to be a conqueror in love, the answer was cryptic: '*My laaitie, is jy 'n moemish? Jy sê A, sy sê B, jy kom met Y and pop! Skoewet under corset* [Boy, are you stupid? You say A, she says B, you go to Y and everything is hunky-dory].'

Having overcome the first hurdle, finding the hay was a much more arduous task. Figure this out: firstly it was taboo for us to even get into the sack. Secondly, considering that the average family had at least four children, and each house had four rooms to house at least six people – assuming

95

no relatives lived there as well – finding space to indulge in the act was well-nigh impossible.

Desperation became the driver of our libidos. To say that finding a stadium (place) to do it was a challenge is an understatement of major proportions. We listened carefully for whose family would be away for the weekend and volunteered to housesit. We befriended widows and the frail in the hope that they would give us caretaking assignments should they go visiting out of town. Of course, when this happened, we made sure that the house was left so clean that any reports of frolicking by neighbours would have no credibility.

First prize was finding a girlfriend who was an only child. This opened up the possibility of the two of you getting together after school when there was no one at her house. The fact that neighbours were generally nosy and ratted on children who got up to mischief was the least of our concerns. If she wasn't an only child, second prize would be for her to have fewer siblings than average, who could easily be shooed away when there were visitors.

Of course, the reverse applied in the case of the boy. And pity the guy who had a stadium. We would beg to borrow it for a few moments. If he agreed, which was not often, synchronising the availability of the stadium and the availability of your conquest was another challenge. And it was not as if you led the willing to the slaughter. MK said that when one such opportunity availed itself, he took his girlfriend to his house. After the customary offer of cool drinks and biscuits, she asked to go to the bathroom. While she was there, MK went into the bathroom and started gyrating suggestively in front of the wall mirror. Unbeknown to him, lover-girl was watching all this unfolding. When he turned, she bolted. And MK could not exactly chase her through the streets of the township, could he?

Tom told of Billy – have you ever noticed that no one tells of their own compromising experiences – having sent an SOS to his friend Montsho that he had a date and nowhere to take her one Sunday afternoon. The ploy was for the couple to arrive at the arranged time and, once the niceties had been dealt with, the host would offer a nebulous reason for leaving the house and thus leave the two to have a go on the sofa. Generally the reason would be, 'Hey Billy, I have run out of cool drink. I am off to get more from the shops.'

Tom said Montsho was hardly out of his house when Montsho called out through the window: '*Hei monna, bowa, re feditse!* [Guy, come back, we have finished!]' I cannot attest to the veracity of this one!

Going on picnics, especially where the spots provided foliage under which the amorous could snuggle, was another solution. Fun Valley, south of Johannesburg, was popular for this reason. Its leafy trees provided groundcover for both mobile and pedestrian visitors to indulge in surreptitious canoodling – and then some more.

When hotels opened to black people, they offered some measure of relief. But Bafana would have none of that. 'You spent 70 bucks on a hotel? I only spent 10 bucks at Fun Valley!' The car-thing was not confined to Fun Valley. Many a young man has lived to tell of being caught in the act on the back seat of a motor vehicle.

I don't know whether to laugh or cry at Papi's tale of woe. Nestled between two trees on a dual carriageway near Baragwanath Hospital one evening, he was blissfully at it when he heard a tap on the window and was blinded by torchlights shining into the car. '*Ja, wat doen julle*? [Yes, what are you doing?],' was the cold Afrikaans question.

'Damn,' Papi tells us. 'This was the middle of the fucking state of emergency and the boers were crawling all over the *kassie*. That's the problem with *phunda* [sex]; it impairs your ability to think. So these soldiers point their R1s (rifles) at us. "*Ja, lekker né*," they teased. I have never begged a white man so much in my life. "Okay, *maak klaar* [finish up]," they commanded. I muffled my protest and heard rifles cocking. We were forced to simulate the act right in front of those fuckers. Only once their sick voyeuristic urges had been satisfied, did they leave us alone.'

This was also the time when the Mixed Marriages Act – which prohibited love across the colour line – was being rigorously enforced by the vice squad. A white colleague says a friend was caught in the car-act by cops. As soon as the cops realised that both parties to the act were white they told my friend: '*Ag sorry, gaan aan. Ons* check *net die kleur* [We beg your pardon; we were just checking whether you were the right colour].'

With the housing situation for blacks being the pits, as we grew older it meant staying at home longer, and often with more additions to the family. So, as Hillbrow slowly opened its rooms to darkies, it provided some relief. Max and Paballo shared a one-bedroom flat and a rather unusual arrangement. Their main condition of cohabitation was simple: if one brought a girl home, the other would have to find lodgings elsewhere that night. Or whoever came home first with a girl was the owner of the flat for that evening. This arrangement, unfortunately, eventually ended the friendship. Today, many moons later, the two are still not on speaking terms.

One Saturday night Paballo arrived home with his conquest in tow. Max, being drunk, refused to make way. Max has the flabby build of a retired, unfit matador, while Paballo owns the physique of the reigning Mr Soweto. Repeated pleas by Paballo for Max to vacate the flat fell on deaf ears. So he was forced to resort to pulverising Max's face with his fists. Now Max wears false teeth, and when we ask him what happened on that fateful evening, he has one consistent answer: 'Paballo is full of shit.'

Tebello

What I know of Irish wakes from the movies is nothing compared with the night vigils in the townships. Whereas, as far as I can make out, the Irish will have a royal mighty piss-up, followed by raucous singing as the mourners get more inebriated, our wakes start as solemn affairs that get more entertaining as the ceremony pushes on through the night. A night vigil typically takes places on the eve of the funeral. It starts anywhere from around 7pm and ends in the wee hours of the morning, generally around 4am.

The religious conviction of the deceased, or their diligence in attending church services and paying their religious dues, dictates whether senior members of the denomination will run the proceedings. The more senior the officiating personnel, the higher the esteem in which the deceased, or a member of their family, is held by the church or community.

A typical vigil starts with a religious service led by the church official and members of the church. It is usually held in a hired tent erected in the deceased's yard. It is attended by all and sundry, in fact anyone who wants to, with only a sprinkling of the deceased's family making up the audience. After the funeral service words of condolence are offered to the bereaved family. And this is where the entertainment starts.

As invariably happens, there will be a shebeen operating all night in close proximity to where the vigil is being held. Or the drunks will have brought enough alcohol, in their tummies and top-ups in their pockets, to last them the night. The early part of the vigil is pretty dignified, with the sober speakers quoting liberally from the Good Book itself. Vigil services are similar to Baptist revivals. One by one the speakers will be roused by song, to testify about the dearly departed whose coffin will be occupying centre stage either in the tent or in the main bedroom.

'Praise the Lord, *bazalwane* [fellow converts],' Bra Joe began as the hymn died down, moved by the spirits he had been furtively imbibing under his coat. 'I have walked many roads met *ou* Willie. Hallelujah!'

'Amen!' responded the audience.

'Hallelujah, *bazalwane*! Oh yes, he was a good man. Each time *ou* Willie and I went to a spot [shebeen], *ek sê 'nip' en hy sê 'nip'* [I bought a nip of brandy, and he would follow suit].'

'*Hei wena*, don't talk like that about someone who has passed away,' the people protested.

'That's the life we lived, what else must I talk about?' Bra Joe replied.

Then a hymn began, and among singing and soulful clapping, Bra Joe was forced to vacate the 'stage', which was really a spot at the front of the tent.

Shortly afterwards, another man took his place on the stage and requested that, before he speak, the audience sing along to his favourite hymn *Sedi la ka mponesetse tsela* [The Lord is my Shepherd]. They duly obliged. '*Tanki, batho ba morena*. Now, before I offer my condolences to the family, please sing my wife's favourite hymn with me, *Joko ea hao e bobebe* [Thy yoke is light].' The audience obliged. '*Tanki, tanki, hape, batho ba morena. Ke ea leboha* [Thank you, praise the Lord]. Now, please, let's sing my daughter's favourite hymn…' He never got to finish the sentence as he was shouted off the stage and another speaker jumped onto the podium, and took over.

Brothers Sello and Matome provided entertainment of another kind. The former neither drank nor smoked. His elder brother, Matome, was exactly the opposite, and depended on his entrepreneurial younger sibling for his existence. As can be expected, whatever Matome did under the influence of alcohol irritated the hell out of Sello. But the two could always be found close together at most vigils. Whenever a hymn was rendered, Matome sang completely out of tune and Sello would castigate him, whispering, '*Hei jy, bly stil. Jy kannie sing* [you can't sing]. You are embarrassing us.'

Between very off-key lines, Matome told his

younger brother, '*Dit is 'n funeral; nie 'n choral competition. Ek sing as ek wil.* [This is a funeral, not a choral competition. I will sing as I please].'

At the vigil of one of our youth club members, a man, not so sure-footed, stood up. '*Batho ba morena* [God's people], I was walking past and I was drawn in by the sorrowful cries in the house of death, hallelujah! Oh, it is such a sad thing when a family loses a mother, the most important member of the household.'

'But it is a child!' the audience corrected him.

'Oh, to lose such an angel. This girl would have grown to help her ageing parents...'

'But it is a boy,' we shouted.

Other titles by Jacana

Beginnings of a Dream
by Zachariah Rapola

How We Buried Puso
by Morabo Morejele

Miss Kwa Kwa
by Stephen Simm

Six Fang Marks and a Tetanus Shot
by Richard de Nooy

Song of the Atman
by Ronnie Govender

Coconut
Kopano Matlwa